J. MACHIEL GALJAARD

The Hague

WITH 48 COLOUR ILLUSTRATIONS
PHOTOGRAPHS BY URSULA PFISTERMEISTER

KNORR & HIRTH VERLAG GMBH
D-3167 AHRBECK/HANNOVER

All rights reserved, in particular of translation and reproduction. Set and printed by WILH. SCHRÖER & CO., *Seelze-Hannover. Binding by* KLEMME & BLEIMUND, *Bielefeld. Blocks by* OSNABRÜCKER KLISCHEEANSTALT, *Osnabrück. Printed in Germany. Published in the series '*THE LITTLE ART BOOK*', edited by* BERTHOLD FRICKE.

© KNORR & HIRTH VERLAG GMBH
1971, 1977
Printed in West Germany
ISBN 3—7821—2105—8

PREFACE

The photographer of this book had never before set eyes on The Hague. Her view of our town should be refreshingly new.

The author, though not a native of the town, confesses his infatuation with The Hague. He has published much on various aspects of the life and history of the town. He preserves an open mind on its vices and virtues and his comments are forthright.

A town, of course, is not a constant. Like human beings, it is subject to a process of change and growth; certain cells deteriorate, others are rejuvenated. Tastes and attitudes tend to change.

A faithful portrait of any city can only maintain its claim to validity if it is continually subject to review. We can stock a library with the books which have been written about The Hague but there is always a demand for more information.

When slides fade and memories become dim, this book will remind the reader what The Hague was like when he was there. It may even inspire the laudable decision to make or renew the acquaintance with our town.

I sincerely hope that we shall see a steady increase in good literature on The Hague. I am aware that good wine needs no bush, but it is always wise to emphasize the truth.

V. G. M. MARIJNEN
Burgomaster of The Hague

If anyone actually takes the trouble to delve into the histories of the major European cities, he will encounter a succession of very similar heroic legends. Vague references to plucky little towns in early times, tales of glorious exploits and prosperity, of tragic sieges and decline. It's like the cycle of men's lives, the same old story all over again.

But appearances are deceptive, and we can glean a lot of interesting information from an ostensibly familiar history. The features of a town tell us how it developed and how, despite all similarity, it became unique.

The Hague is unique in this country because it was never constricted by walls and intersected by canals like other ancient Dutch towns. Its situation on the border of polders and sandy rises favoured its development on a generous scale, rare in Holland, that can be safely called European; an impression that is fortified by countless architectural reminiscences of royal residences elsewhere in Europe. The ancient court capital of the counts of Holland forms the heart of the modern town of The Hague which is at once cosmopolitan and unmistakably Dutch. Pomp and display are tempered by characteristic Dutch sobriety and frugality.

The original and still the official name of the town is 's-Gravenhage, deriving from an obsolete genitive "des Graven Hage" or the Count's Park. Early records already mention an alternative version 'In der Haghe' which has developed into the commonly used present-day form 'Den Haag'. This name translates in practically all languages: The Hague, La Haye, Hag, Haga, Haag, l'Aya.

Towns are like people. All are alike yet each is unique, and character-istic features are accentuated by age. That is why old towns are so attractive to tourists. There is a lyrical quality in their appeal, not easily captured in words, that is akin to music.

This music echoes in age-old precincts but it resounds no less in the modern commercial centres, though many people fail to appreciate the fact. A sympathetic observer or listener inquires into the whys and hows. History can fill him in on this. So let's take a glance at the history of The Hague. In Roman times there was a naval base in the vicinity of the site of the present town. The region consequently had a high population density for the time. Little has survived, however, of the Roman settlement. There is an ancient waterway, the Vliet, still running its unruffled course through the polders east of The Hague, which was presumably cut by the Roman commander Corbulo to provide a sheltered passage for his galleys. Present-day motorists barely notice it as they dash past on the highway that forms the eastern approach to The Hague. The modern main roads still follow the same routes constructed by the Romans round The Hague, running parallel to the coast across the low sandhills or at right-angles to it by the shortest route through the fens. At some time between the 4th and 6th centuries a fishing hamlet developed on the coast. This was the later village of Scheveningen which therefore has older papers than The Hague. Despite the lack of actual records, the presence of this community of offshore fishermen indicates a fairly well-populated hinter-land, for it is reasonable to suppose that the fishermen must have been able to sell their fish at some not too far distant place.

The origin of The Hague, records show, goes back to 1248. In that year William II, Count of Holland, commenced the construction of a palace at the site of his hunting-lodge on the banks of a clear lake in the dunes. The historic landmark and environs have survived to this day. The ornamental Hofvijver (Court Lake) in the heart of the modern town is all that remains of the former wild lake. And on its banks we find the count's palace on the Binnenhof (Inner Court), where it is tucked away among the parliament buildings beyond the famous Ridderzaal (Knights' Hall).

A mediæval count was always on the move, travelling from town to town to administrate his domains. William's ancestors had never counted a palace among their possessions in Holland. The most they could manage was a fortress or two. But by a trick of fate our William was elected King of the Holy Roman Empire, and he naturally had to live up to his exalted station. In the event, this had far-reaching consequences for The Hague, the village that had sprung up at the gates of the new palace. For The Hague became, and has since remained, the seat of ruler and government of the Low Countries in the delta of the Rhine.

William's son, Floris V (1256—1296), extended his power and added to his already considerable fortune, in particular by selling his claims to the throne of Scotland. He built the Ridderzaal when his father's Hall became too modest for his tastes. The growing prosperity of ruler and subjects was reflected in the surroundings. Fine houses made their appearance on the shores of the lake. The wooden structures on Buitenhof (Forecourt) and Plaats (Place), both of them well-known squares in present-day The Hague, were supplanted by buildings in red and yellow brick. Some of these are still extant, the most notable being the forbidding mediæval gatehouse prison, the Gevangenpoort.

But there were many open spaces left. The successive counts of Holland jealously guarded their private woodland game runs, the pleasance on the far side of the lake where courtiers frolicked and gambolled (Vijverberg), the great quadrangle of the kitchen-gardens (now Het Plein), and the spacious wooded park (Voorhout) where summer visitors were put up in large tents.

The early rulers of Holland determined the friendly open character of their Residence by putting a curb on excessive building and refraining from the construction of a walled stronghold with moats and ramparts. Citizens of fortified towns were expected to foot the bill of the costly fortifications, the price of ground rising in proportion to the strength of the defences. At The Hague, however, extensive — though admittedly unprotected — properties were available at a relatively low price right next-door to the count himself. In other Dutch towns, with rates based on frontage, houses tended to be tall and narrow whereas building was possible on a much grander scale at The Hague at the same cost. This certainly suited the display-loving residents of the court capital, among them many members of the landed aristocracy who had deserted their country seats to join the court.

The Hague flourished, but it was just a village at the palace gates for all that. Duke Albert of Bavaria, regent of Holland in the mid-14th century, considered the parish church quite unsuitable for the nuptials of his daughter. So he added a choir that would have done justice to a cathedral.

Though pigs still grubbed about on the Buitenhof and the arrival of visitors sent chickens flying on the Binnenhof, innkeepers, curriers, lace-makers, and other men of trade were conducting a thriving business. The Hague was definitely on the make.

The village became exceedingly prosperous indeed. In the early 16th century the Cardinal of Aragon wrote: "We found a village without canals, as lovely as one can hope to find anywhere in the world. It bears comparison with any fine big town." And fifty years later Ludovico Guicciardini, a Florentine nobleman, recorded: "This is, I venture to say, the prettiest, richest, and largest open village on the continent. There are more than a thousand dwellings, many of them extremely grand, and a magnificent royal palace."

Every town, alas, has its ups and downs. The Hague was in luck until the mid-16th century. It was sacked on only one occasion and even then the major part of the booty was ransomed. But the rebellion of the Low Countries against their Spanish overlord, Philip II, ushered in a reign of terror. The unfortified town suffered severely at the hands of the belligerents in the chronic struggle that followed. The Court had moved elsewhere and those who could afford to sought refuge with their goods and chattels in neighbouring fortified towns. The streets were soon infested with weeds and the Grote Kerk was converted into stables.

When the fortunes of war turned and the Golden Age dawned upon the country, The Hague became the seat of government of the powerful 17th-century Republic of the United Provinces. There was a tremendous influx of wealth and canals were constructed to protect the residents against robbers rather than from defensive considerations. Numerous fine houses and churches still bear witness to the flowering of the period. Frenzied building activities were conducted from the mid-17th century through the 18th century. Nobles and wealthy patricians vied with each other in pulling down mediæval structures and replacing them by larger and grander mansions in a style that reflected the latest European fashions in architecture adapted to the Dutch taste.

Every age has its status symbols. We have our second car, our yacht or swimming-pool. Our ancestors may have had their farms or a country-house, but the real status symbol of the 18th century was the wrought-iron scroll-work of railings, lanterns, and fanlights.

The lovely doorway shown here is a detail in a fine row of façades on one of the canals. The residents of these houses had, and still have, a view of a wide stretch of turf on the far side of the canal. This is the Malieveld which once lay beyond the town limits. By the 18th century, when these houses were built, the field had lost its original purpose. Since the Middle Ages, the game of 'malie' or 'kolf', in which a ball was struck by a stick, was played here by the nobles. Lost in oblivion for many years, the sport returned to this country in modern times as the British game of golf. Beyond the field lies the Haagse Bos, the age-old Hague Wood bordering on the dunes, which has been a highly valued amenity of the town since time immemorial. In 1565, the practically penniless Town Council actually sold the bells of St. Jacob's to avert a scheme for cutting down the wood. The present north road into town skirts the Wood and Malieveld and brings us face to face with this harmonious row of houses on Prinsessegracht. From afar we see their windows lightening under the vast Dutch sky.

4. PRINSESSEGRACHT
(PRINCESSES' CANAL)
Doorway of a House

In the history of every country there are dark pages marred by out-
bursts of inconceivable brutality. Later generations may erect memo-
rials but they can never expunge the blots.

On the historic Plaats in front of the Binnenhof is a monument to John
de Witt, one of the greatest statesmen of the United Provinces. He had
incurred the hatred of the people at a time of severe political tension
and when he visited his brother who was confined in the Gevangenpoort, the mediæval prison on the Plaats, he was dragged out of the
building and brutally murdered by the mob. The famous Dutch philosopher Spinoza, a normally undemonstrative man, was beside himself
when he heard of the outrage. Shaking with anger, he scrawled on a
sheet of paper: 'Ultimi Barbarorum' (The last of the barbarians). He
would have dashed out to post it up at the scene of the crime if his
host, fearing that his rashness would cost him his life, had not taken
the precaution to lock him in. The monument itself is not particularly
important, but the story of the dramatic events it symbolizes makes
the tourist alive to the atmosphere of the surroundings and teaches him
something about the history of the town.

A sharp-eyed observer will detect a sandstone slab marked with
seven notches among the square tiles at the foot of de Witt's statue.
Hereby hangs another tale. A frivolous lady at the mediæval court
indulged in a mild flirtation with political overtones with the regent,
Duke Albert. She was set upon by her political rivals and the blows
of their swords mark the spot where she was struck down. The present
writer is not prepared to vouch for the veracity of incident and place.
But he has no qualms about doing so for the standards and safety of
the agreeable shopping precinct which extends from the Plaats through
a sizable part of the city centre.

5. PLAATS (PLACE)

If you walk a mile or two away from Scheveningen at dusk, you'll find yourself alone on a deserted beach, the low range of dunes behind you and the sea stretching away to the horizon ahead; firm sand underfoot flattened by the rollers, with the scattered remains of marine life which are thrown ashore and washed away in the endless rhythm of ebb and flow.

But modern man, it seems, has no taste for solitude or raw nature, except perhaps in minute doses by way of contrast to his affluent life. He will admire the magnificent sunsets at Scheveningen, where the sun goes down in a mass of blue and fiery cloud, but preferably in the company of others. He likes holiday crowds, myriads of twinkling lights, and the flashy slogans of a publicity-conscious society. He wants music and movement, anything to forget his insignificance in the face of nature. Which is something best left to space travellers.

That is why modern seaside resorts are like huge playgrounds packed with every imaginable form of garish amusement. And why resort life is a sophisticated social affair where carefree holiday-makers flock together, staring and stared at as they lounge about in every state of dress and undress, basking in the sun or relaxing in the cool of the evening, doing sweet nothing.

8. SCHEVENINGEN
The Promenade by Night

Pictures of harbours are never quite satisfactory. One misses the pervasive tang of pitch and tar and fish, the sound of engines thudding and chains rattling on a deck.

The harbour of Scheveningen is primarily a fishing-port, the second largest in the country, but it handles an increasing amount of carrying trade and there is a regular ferry service to Britain.

The harbour is of comparatively recent date, having been constructed in the early years of the century. The Scheveningen fishers formerly sailed in small, squat, but extremely sturdy vessels which were capable of riding through the surf in much the same way as the Hovercraft does today. It was a ticklish business though, sailing as they did on a stiff breeze with no protective air-cushion between ship and sea. The Mesdag Panorama at The Hague shows how it was done and in late-19th-century seascapes we see the flat-bottomed craft drawn up on the shore.

Later on the fishing fleet sailed further afield in larger, safer, and swifter boats. The harbour was constructed and basins were added as the need arose. Scheveningen is a well-equipped fishing-port and there is a large up-to-date fish-market which bustles with activity at what ordinary mortals consider an unearthly hour. Cold-storage warehouses and canneries abound in and around the port. Fishing gear has been modernized; steel has supplanted wood, steam and diesel engines have taken over from sails, nylon has replaced rope. But deep-sea fishing is still a pretty hazardous undertaking and very much of a gamble.

9. SCHEVENINGEN
The Harbour

Latest creations of fashion are more in evidence at Scheveningen now-adays than traditional costume. But Scheveningen is one of the few places in the country where costumes are still worn at all. You can see them if you stroll through the old fishing village and you may even run into a costumed woman in down-town The Hague.

The fishing community of Scheveningen has always been a close, tightly knit group, demonstrating its reserve by wearing a distinctive dress. The women wear long black skirts with smoothly ironed black or blue aprons and black or brightly coloured shawls. The headdress consists of a white cambric cap worn over a gold or silver 'ear iron'. This is a broad metal band fitting closely round the head and terminating over the ears in oblong plates known as the 'books'. The gold or silver band can be seen glittering under the cap which is fastened with ornamental pins in the same precious metal. The traditional costume has its conventions and even fashions, barely perceptible, however, to outsiders.

Our photo shows Scheveningen women in front of their lovely old parish church. Once upon a time this church stood in the centre of the village. But the dike, forming the present esplanade, now rises directly behind it, the intervening ground having been engulfed by the sea long ago. An imposing number of authentic Scheveningen costumes are mustered here at church-time on Sundays. The severe black and dark blue of the men relieved by the dazzling white of the women's crisply starched caps make a charming picture.

10. SCHEVENINGEN
Costumes

*A view of sea and shore, fresh water, and well-stocked game preserves
— that is what Count William II of Holland must have had in mind,
looking for a place where he could retire between campaigns.*

He found the place of his dreams at the site that later became The
Hague. Once upon a time he must have stood on the dunes near the
town looking down at the sea and the beach. But definitely not at the
spot shown in the illustration. This is actually a detail from the Mesdag Panorama which attracts thousands of visitors every year. From
a central platform the spectators view the enormous seascape, 1700
square metres of it, painted on a cylindrical surface round them to
create an illusion of reality. But the waves do not roll, the fluttering
pennants are still, the cavalry on the beach are arrested in a petrified
gallop, not a single cloud moves in the dome of the sky, and the only
sound is the shuffling of visitors' feet.

The Panorama is probably the most entertaining picture on view
at The Hague. It was commissioned from the 19th-century painter
Willem Mesdag by a Belgian firm in 1891. Mesdag enlisted the aid of
a few other artists. G. H. Breitner executed the cavalry, Th. de Bock
the clouds, H. Blommers the figures, and Mesdag's wife the village.
When his patron failed in business, Mesdag, who was the scion of a
wealthy banking family, acquired the spectacular work and installed
it in a specially constructed building where it still is today. Some of
the older residents of Scheveningen visit the Panorama at least once
a year to refurbish their memories of the past.

11. THE MESDAG PANORAMA

The complex of buildings on the Hofvijver has its origins in the Middle Ages. This is evident in its general aspect, despite haphazard building activities of later times.

Many buildings have special historical associations: the residence of Countess Margaret of Savoy, regent of the Low Countries in the early decades of the 16th century; the quarters of the Earl of Leicester; the tower apartment of the brilliant soldier Prince Maurice, second Prince of Orange; the Trèves Hall which derives its name (trève = truce) from the peace talks held here in 1648 to negotiate the treaty by which Spain finally acknowledged the independence of the Netherlands after eighty years of intermittent warfare.

The Hague is inordinately proud of the majestic edifice which preens in floodlit magnificence on summer nights. However, it is not just a decorative and historic landmark. As seat of Parliament where both legislative chambers assemble, it is the hub of Dutch political life. Though several ministries have moved to modern steel and glass constructions elsewhere, many government officials still enjoy the privilege of working in this delightful environment in the very heart of the town, overlooking the placid pool that is disturbed only occasionally by an irate hissing of swans or a quacking commotion on the duck island. — As one saunters along the crunching gravel walks, watching the inevitable anglers and the trim secretaries sharing their lunch with gliding gulls, it seems incredible that this is the centre of a conurbation that shelters a million souls.

16. THE MAURITSHUIS
on the Hofvijver

*No motorist would dream of parking his car on the central avenue of
the Lange Voorhout even if there was not an inch of space to spare in
the entire neighbourhood. One vehicle is allowed here once a year;
and that is the Gold Coach in which the Queen drives in state to per-
form the annual opening of Parliament.*

Since time immemorial, foreign envoys and wealthy patricians have
resided on the Lange Voorhout to which long rows of stately shade
trees lend an air of almost rural quiet. Encroaching business firms of
a later period discreetly maintain a style appropriate to the distinguished surroundings.

The good old Dutch barrel-organ, however, is undeterred by such
niceties. Parking his instrument four-square on the walk that is carefully avoided by passing traffic, the organ-grinder lustily produces a
cheerful cascade of sound as the wheezy warbling tones reverberate
between the trees and walls. The peaceful atmosphere is also shattered
on occasion by the din of street fairs in spring and autumn. With a
sublime disregard of starched gentility, the whole town turns out to
join in the popular merry-making on the Voorhout.

17. THE VOORHOUT
with a Barrel-Organ

"In no other town, not even in the Faubourg Saint-Germain, did I feel such a poor devil as in these districts. The broad, straight streets are flanked by little palaces which are pleasing in form and bright in colour, with large unshuttered windows affording a view of carpets, vases, and priceless furniture in the downstairs rooms."

This was the impression of a foreign visitor, Edmondo de Amicis, in 1873. He continued in the same strain: "All doors are shut, and there's no shop, no street sign, no nook or alley to be seen though you looked with a hundred eyes. A deep silence reigned when I walked through the streets. Only at rare intervals did I encounter an aristocratic coach rolling soundlessly over brick-paved streets or see a footman standing like a statue in front of a house or a fair woman's head at a window. As I passed by the windows, I stole a glance at my shabby travelling costume mercilessly reflected in the large panes of glass and regretted the fact that I went ungloved."

This, of course, is past history. Present-day visitors have no reason to bewail the shortage of shops at The Hague and the streets in the metropolitan area are bright with flashing neon signs. The solitary coach has given way to the press of traffic. But the stately mansions which aroused the gentleman's admiration are still with us, the same shiny windows affording a view of luxurious furnishings which may even be the same he saw.

Our illustration shows the former residence of the great 17th-century statesman Johan de Witt, which is still the scene of brilliant official receptions hold by local or government boards.

18. THE JOHN DE WITT MANSION on the Kneuterdijk

The Voorhout was at all times a much desired residential address for people of rank and fortune and that may be why it has remained one of the loveliest avenues in the country.

The magnificent house shown here was built by Daniel Marot, in 1735, for the heiress Marguerite de Huguetan, daughter of a French banker who had helped to finance Louis XIV's campaigns, when she married a descendant of the great Prince Maurice late in life.

The great and gracious mansion was fit for a king. And for a short time it was indeed the residence of the first sovereign of the Kingdom of the Netherlands. In 1819 King William I donated the mansion to the state together with his priceless collection of books, which forms the nucleus of the present Royal Library. The holdings of the library, ranging from illuminated mediæval manuscripts to the latest academic thesis, fill thirty kilometres of shelving. The former ball-room is doubt-less the most attractive public reading-room in The Hague.

19. THE ROYAL LIBRARY

Glittering gilt scroll-work decorates the mansion commanding a view of the Voorhout, which is still popularly known as the Queen Mother's Palace in memory of Queen Juliana's grandmother, the revered Queen Emma, who acted as regent during the minority of Queen Wilhelmina.

The lacy wrought-iron railings and the gilt coronets on the ancient gas lamps are nostalgic reminders of a bygone era when liveried lackeys stood bowing at the foot of the steps as they opened carriage-doors for ladies in crinolines.

Not built as a royal residence but as a banker's town house, the mansion was chosen to lodge an emperor. For Napoleon stayed here when he visited The Hague in 1813.

Hague architecture was always lavishly elegant and stylish, reflecting the rivalry of permanent and temporary residents, of courtiers and diplomats, who competed in pomp and splendour. We consequently find a wide range of styles rather than one particular style; this eclecticism, in fact, is regarded as characteristic of The Hague. The French-born architect Daniel Marot, who came to Holland as a young refugee, was particularly active at The Hague. He achieved a skilful compromise between the magnificence of the French neo-classical style and the sobriety of the native Dutch style. In two generations' time he and his brother architects practically eradicated the last vestiges of mediæval architecture at The Hague. Step- and bell-gables succumbed under the inroads of the latest architectural fancies of the 18th century.

20. THE VOORHOUT
Royal Residence

The old and narrow little streets, once designed to give passage to nothing larger than a horseman or a sledge, have been turned into a sequence of shopping precincts.

The Hague has always made it its business to cater for the needs of shoppers. The presence of the Court in early days offered excellent opportunities to skilled craftsmen. Embroiderers and lacemakers, tailors and milliners, glovers, curriers and shoemakers, cutlers and saddlers, supplied the luxuries demanded by discerning patrons. The fame of their superb craftsmanship spread far beyond the relatively small circle of aristocratic customers and The Hague acquired an early reputation as an elegant shopping centre.

The elegance is as much in evidence as ever, despite the radical changes of the present era in which workshops are transformed into boutiques, markets are supplanted by palatial department stores, and acres of plate glass disrupt the old-world image of the townscape. Fashion collections display an unmistakable chic and the sophisticated smartness we invariably associate with the town is unique in Holland.   21. Spuistraat

For reasons that are not always clear shops selling the same commodities have a tendency to cluster together. Trade attracts trade, so common interest may be the bond. Art and antique shops, always a major attraction in tourist centres, are often concentrated in one area.

Dealers in antiques, old prints, and other objects of art usually pitch their tents in the immediate neighbourhood of the sight-seeing centres, preferable in easily accessible but intimate little side streets where treasure hunters can wander at will.

The Hague is no exception in this respect. In the area around the elbow of the Voorhout, in the vicinity of the Binnenhof or the Grote Kerk, there is rich hunting-ground which visitors will be well advised to explore. But the skilled treasure hunter doesn't need to be told where to look. He only has to follow his nose to pick up the most marvellous bargains wherever he goes.

22. THE DENNEWEG
An Antique Shop

The Heilige-Geesthofje was founded in 1616 by the Guardians of the Poor of the Grote or St. Jacobskerk to house the paupers in the care of the parish.

Many people no doubt lived in a state of extreme poverty in the fabulously rich Holland of the 17th century. But there was also a surprisingly effective provision for the poor and destitute. We are inclined to scoff at the baskets of peat, potatoes, and other benefits in kind that were doled out by the parish to old ladies in reduced circumstances. But this form of bounty can only be judged fairly in the context of the time when commodities were in any case easier to dispense than cash.

Privately endowed charitable foundations, inspired perhaps by the wish of some wealthy patrician to make (and pay for) his peace with God or to perpetuate the fame of his name, were common in the country. They were often established for a specially designated group of persons, members of a particular family, widows of soldiers, etc. The almshouses were usually built around an enclosed courtyard, for no one cared to flaunt his poverty or age. The Heilige-Geesthofje at The Hague is one of the most charming almshouses in the country. It has been preserved in exquisite state by the good care of the Governors. The cottages, with all conveniences, are highly desirable dwellings.

23. HEILIGE-GEESTHOFJE
(Holy Ghost Court)

The four-square elegance of the Mauritshuis dominates one end of the Hofvijver. The palatial mansion was built, in the mid-17th century, for Count John Maurice of Nassau-Siegen who had amassed a fortune in Brazil, where he served as governor of the Dutch colonies.

The house was constructed under the direction of the famous architect Pieter Post to the design of his great predecessor Jacob van Campen during the Count's absence in Brazil. It took ten years to complete. The Count regularly shipped home cargoes of sugar to defray the costs of his mansion, promptly dubbed "the Sugar Palace", and exotic treasures for its embellishment. His housewarming party certainly struck an exotic note, a band of naked "savages" performing a dance which long remained the talk of the town. Count John Maurice only lived here for a relatively brief period; able administrators were in great demand and in 1647 he took up an appointment as governor of Cleve, Mark, and Ravensburg. The lavishly furnished Mauritshuis was frequently used to lodge visiting royalty.

When the king's picture collection was transferred to the mansion in the early 19th century, it acquired its present name: The Royal Cabinet of Paintings "Mauritshuis". The Mauritshuis, with approximately a thousand pictures, is a relatively small museum. Owing to the high quality of its holdings, however, it ranks as one of the major museums in the world. The exceptionally fine collection of 17th-century Dutch and Flemish masters includes 14 works by Rembrandt, 13 by Jan Steen, 3 by Vermeer, 3 by Van Dyck, and 7 by Rubens, just to mention a few. — The Mauritshuis represents an essential aspect of this town and this country. A visit there is an absolute must.

24. THE MAURITSHUIS

The Mauritshuis is but a stone's throw from the Binnenhof, seat of the federal authority of the mighty Dutch Republic of the Golden Age. The eminent situation emphasizes the prestige of the man who built the palatial mansion.

The fine sundial in the forecourt was added at a later date. In fact, the paved courtyard and wrought-iron railings replaced the original trellised garden which was connected by a subway with the spacious grounds on the far side of the road, where guests strolled and chatted in shady arbours.

The gardens have vanished. Gone, also, is the moat that once encircled the entire Binnenhof and the bridge that resounded with the rumbling of coaches. But the roofs, battlements, and turrets of the ancient palace of the Counts of Holland still tower above the fine old archway in very much the same manner as in days gone by. The old-world atmosphere that pervades this neighbourhood in the very heart of The Hague is absolutely authentic.

25. VIEW OF THE BINNENHOF
from the Mauritshuis

*One of the pictures hanging in this room may well be a museum direc-
tor's despair. Though an untold number of visitors stare at in spell-
bound admiration, one has misgivings on the score.*

The large picture (2.5 by 4.5 metres), popularly known as "Potter's
Bull", shows a herdsman with a young bull and some cows and sheep.
It was painted, in 1647, by the well-known animal painter Paul Potter.
The work is uncannily realistic, painstakingly recording every single
hair, leaf, or blade of grass. The handling is extremely skilful, but
literal description does not necessarily produce a great work of art.
And in any case there are many pictures in the collection of the
Mauritshuis which are far superior to this spectacular work in quality
and emotional appeal.

Every person is naturally entitled to his likes and dislikes. A
Spanish journalist who found "the Bull" irresistible gave the following
interpretation of the picture: "I'm afraid that many Dutchmen fail to
appreciate Potter's Bull because their eyes are accustomed to the tame
domestic cattle of their country. Dutch bulls admittedly sire prime
dairy cattle but they never sired offspring with a muzzle as defiant as
this one. And it is this muzzle, I fear, that puts off the Dutch who do
not like bull-fights. This bull was obviously born to waylay Manolete
(the famous toreador)."

The Mauritshuis has been styled the greatest little museum in the
world. Though it is indeed small, with all the important pictures
assembled in fifteen rooms, the consistently high quality of the holdings
justifies its claim to a place among the world's great museums. The
compact survey highlights the achievements and fosters an understand-
ing of the Dutch painters in the Golden Age.

26. MAURITSHUIS
Interior with 'Potter's Bull'

We only know thirty-six pictures by Johannes Vermeer of Delft who died at the age of forty-three. They rank, however, among the greatest works that have come down to us from the Golden Age. The 'View of Delft' showing the artist's native town is one of the most famous out of this small selection.

Due to its hanging in the gallery, the amazingly serene picture shows a perceptible change of mood corresponding with every change of weather, season or light.

Johannes Vermeer belongs to the third generation of painters of the 17th-century Dutch School. He was second to none in the manipulation of space and the mastery of the problems of light and colour which has made this School famous throughout the world.

The artist, who was also an art dealer, apparently enjoyed renown and esteem in his lifetime (1632–1675). Collectors travelled from as far as France to visit him. He was virtually forgotten after his death until he was rescued from oblivion in the 19th century. Captivated by this picture in the Mauritshuis, the French journalist and art critic Etienne-Joseph-Théophile Thoré (pseudonym: 'W. Bürger') was indefatigable in his search for work that could possibly be attributed to the artist. A review of his findings by later critics has ultimately left us the exceedingly small but exquisite œuvre we now know.

Experts are unanimous in their praise of the superb technical mastery of Vermeer who was probably a slow and circumspect worker. Some people think that he may have used a *camera obscura* for sketching the preliminary studies of this picture in which topographers recognize the spires of the Oude and the Nieuwe Kerk and the Schiedam and Rotterdam Gates on the banks of the Schie. But the fascination of the work lies in the evocation of silence, the pervasive mood of tranquillity, which renders the spectator oblivious to his surroundings.

27. MAURITSHUIS
VERMEER, 'VIEW OF DELFT'

Jan Steen, who has several pictures in the Mauritshuis, occupies a rather special place among the painters of the Golden Age. Though unmistakably Dutch, he demonstrates an un-characteristic, whimsical attitude; keen observation of character is paired with a waggish sense of humour which has often been misunderstood.

He has been charged with being a dissolute rake. Considering the sheer size of his œuvre, this seems highly improbable. The French journalist and critic Thoré-Bürger rightly regarded him as a portrayer of "le genre humain", the human species, and ranking as such with Molière.

Apart from the cheerfully vulgar peasant scenes commonly associated with him, Jan Steen also tackled religious themes. He painted seventy biblical scenes representing a fifth of his total output. But true to type, six of these were devoted to the Wedding at Cana and not a single one to the Agony in the Garden.

28. MAURITSHUIS
JAN STEEN, THE OYSTER-EATER

"The composition holds no mysteries and riddles. At first glance it suggests unpremeditated directness, but the simplicity is the simplicity of genius." Observing this portrait of a child, which is one of the latest acquisitions of the Mauritshuis, we are inclined to agree with the above characteristic of the work of the 17th-century painter Frans Hals.

No other artist among the Titan race of Old Dutch Masters can compare with Hals in facility of composition and execution. Even the awkward plane of the medallion on which our laughing boy is painted has not induced a contrived and cramped design. The strokes are brushed on vigorously and with apparently effortless accuracy.

Frans Hals enjoyed a considerable contemporary reputation because of work like this. His studies were copied on an extensive scale, but with what a world of difference compared to the brilliantly free handling of the originals. Later on his work went out of fashion. In the 19th century we find his rather boisterous studies dismissed as 'unpolished'. In the event, appreciation of the work of the Impressionists led to a re-assessment of Hals's superb talent. Recognizing the impressionist spontaneity and directness in the work of this outstanding artist, the present-day spectator is tempted to conclude that Hals was two hundred years ahead of his time. But that is only of secondary importance. What really matters is that we experience the undiminished vitality of the work and the magic of a great master reaching out to us across the gap of the ages.

29. MAURITSHUIS
FRANS HALS,
PORTRAIT OF A CHILD

Rembrandt's last self portrait is not the most dramatic picture by the renowned 17th-century artist in the Mauritshuis collection, but it is undoubtedly one of the most penetrating.

The great master of the Dutch Golden Age has left us at least sixty portraits of himself. This is characteristic of the universal artist who was one of the greatest and most original talents in Europe and whose concern was truth rather than beauty. It must have been this restless quest for truth that impelled him time and again to study his own image in the mirror with a soul-searching scrutiny. The sequence of self portraits provides a documentary of Rembrandt's life and marks the evolution of his personality and his art.

The versatile artist explored practically every aspect of Dutch art. Portraits and portrait groups had already established his reputation as a young man (e. g. 'The Anatomy Lesson of Dr. Tulp' in the Mauritshuis). He painted one hundred and sixty biblical themes (e. g. the dramatically beautiful double portrait 'David and Saul', also in the museum). Six hundred of his paintings, three hundred etchings, and two thousand drawings have come down to us. The drawings are in many instances an artistic short-hand in which he recorded everything that caught his attention. Several of these are on view in the rather somnolent little Bredius Museum.

30. MAURITSHUIS
REMBRANDT, SELF PORTRAIT

All Hague museums originated as private collections assembled with great dedication by men of taste in an earlier age. They have fortunately retained something of the original atmosphere. Relatively small and intimate, they reflect the individual preferences of the collectors.

There is ample evidence of this in the collections of the Municipal Museum. The museum itself is quite large but the various departments are actually museums in their own right.

The Department of Modern Art provides an illuminating survey of the development of contemporary Dutch art in relation to the great international currents. The Decorative Arts Department has extremely fine collections of China and Delftware and of antique and modern glass. The Music Department, with a large collection of exotic and old European instruments and an important collection of manuscript scores, is one of the best in Europe. The number of playable antique instruments is unique. The Historical Department shows delightful local interiors which transport us back to grandmother's day. The effect is fortunately not marred by the harsh rectangular lines of the windows. The up-to-date museum, which provides special facilities for children, is an important civic cultural centre and it organizes a wide range of events throughout the year.

31. Het Gemeentemuseum
The Municipal Museum
(Architect H. P. Berlage, 1955)

79

A group of painters was active at The Hague in the mid-19th century. Though characterized by a distinctive tone, the work of this so-called Hague School was closely related with contemporary Impressionism. The seascape with fishing-boat by Jacob Maris which is shown in the Municipal Museum is a fine and typical example of the work of this School of The Hague.

The painters of the Hague School were obsessed by light. They did not roam the polders and dunes round The Hague to observe the cows, the flat pasturelands, the waterways or the sea, but to study the effects of light on cows, meadows and water, and to explore the silvery light above the sea and shore. Compared with the French Impressionists, their tonal values were restrained, for the light pervading the Dutch landscape is less vivid than the light of France. Their handling of landscape is in the best tradition of their great predecessors, but their brushwork is broader and more vigorous, particularly in conveying a response to atmosphere.

Work of the Hague School can be seen in the Mesdag Museum and the Mesdag Panorama, both initiated by one of the leaders of the School. And several pictures of this School form the starting-point of the Municipal Museum's large collection of modern art, among them the *bomschip* (a flat-bottomed Scheveningen fishing-boat specially constructed to be run up on the beach) painted by Jacob Maris.

32. HET GEMEENTEMUSEUM
The Municipal Museum
JACOB MARIS, FISHING-BOAT
on the Shore at Scheveningen

The Municipal Museum has the largest collection in the world of the famous artist Piet Mondrian. His work, all too often dismissed as "mere squares and lines", does not meet with universal appreciation.

Piet Mondrian (1872–1944) tried to represent the reality of form and space as a geometrical abstraction. His aim, in other words, was to achieve an ideal harmony in a flat plane. His later work was the inevitable consequence of early experiments. The Municipal Museum shows an extremely interesting sequence of studies demonstrating how the fragmented forms of a tree were transformed into a purely abstract linear arrangement which has its intrinsic laws and an intrinsic beauty.

Apart from the retrospective survey of Mondrian's cool art, visitors to the Museum can follow the development of modern art from the 19th century until the present day. But the Museum caters for a wide variety of interests as we have remarked in a previous note. In addition to the permanent collections, special exhibitions are frequently arranged of contemporary art or treasures of the past from every part of the world.

33. HET GEMEENTEMUSEUM
The Municipal Museum
PART OF THE
MONDRIAN COLLECTION

As long ago as 1518, a foreign visitor to The Hague already remarked on the eye-catching women of the town. The Hague was always a pace-maker of fashion in this country and the Costume Museum presents a pageant of Dutch fashion throughout the ages.

It is the dress of the sophisticated man or woman of fashion that claims our attention here, not the traditional local costumes. The charm of this museum is that you do not walk between showcases filled with costumed figures. You re-enter a vanished world, the drawing-room, dining-room, linen-room or kitchen of some grand house in the 18th or 19th century. The spacious rooms are arranged with authentic furniture, upholstery, carpets, and hangings. In fact, the visitor is the only foreign element in the period surroundings of this 'Cabinet of fashion and good taste'. The light is rather dim and mysterious, but there is a very practical reason for that. Daylight would be ruinous to the fragile materials. The light actually strengthens the illusion of stepping back in time.

Our forebears may have been pretty but, judging by the garments shown here, they must have been small and slight. Few of our well-developed modern young amazons can wear these clothes and it's always a problem to find mannequins when the museum puts on a show of past fashion.

The French philosopher Denis Diderot, who visited The Hague in 1774, was not impressed by the local ladies. "I know", he recorded, "that I only saw ugly women. The men, as a rule, are well but heavily built." So many men so many minds. Fortunately for our Hague ladies a British naval officer discovered "squares crowded with ladies, who rendered this town more agreeable than we had first imagined".

34. HET KOSTUUMMUSEUM
The Costume Museum

Hendrik Willem Mesdag was one of the most picturesque personalities among the artists who worked at The Hague. He had a good head for business (which is rare for an artist) and he was a discerning collector. He has left a whole museum full of pictures.

Born as the son of a banker, in 1831, Mesdag entered the family firm. He was determined, however, to become a painter and at the age of thirty-five he renounced the world of finance to pursue a career in art. With his wife, who was also a painter, he left for Brussels where they worked with several artists. He was remarkably successful from the outset. He won an award with a seascape and his work found a ready market. Not, it must be admitted, without some judicious pushing on his side. He had a trick of bidding on his own work at auctions, un-blushingly describing his paintings as masterpieces, when the bidding was too low for his liking.

In France Mesdag became acquainted with the new style of the artists who were the precursors of Impressionism: Corot, Courbet, Millet, and Daubigny. He bought their pictures and had a house spe-cially built for the collection. Mesdag was accustomed to rent any room affording a view of a scene he particularly wanted to paint. He then proceeded to chalk out the sketch of his picture on the window-pane, a habit which earned him a certain notoriety among the chamber-maids of Scheveningen hotels.

Mesdag was a generous and amiable man and for many years the leader of the artists' society Pulchri Studio. We have already men-tioned his Panorama of late-19th-century Scheveningen which is still one of the popular attractions of The Hague. But the atmosphere of the period is particularly well preserved in the cheerful tranquillity of the Mesdag Museum with its polished floors.

35. The Mesdag Museum

The third Prince of Orange who ruled as Stadholder of the United Republic did not seem over-eager to be married. Campaigning in summer and the diversions of the court at The Hague in winter kept him busy and happy. And when the merry Prince Charming, who had been brought up by his French mother, took himself a wife at last, the marriage seemed dictated by reason.

Prince Frederick Henry married a lady-in-waiting of the exiled Queen of Bohemia, daughter of James I of England, who lived at The Hague for many years. He married for love and his young wife, who shared his tastes and interests, was devoted to him. The couple lived in splendid style. The austere military simplicity of the Stadholder's Quarter on the Hofvijver accorded ill with their way of life and they built two magnificent country houses, one in the polders and another in the dunes, both now demolished.

It was much later that the Prince decided to build his dear Amalia a villa in the Hague Wood. Pieter Post, one of the ablest architects in the country, was entrusted with the design of the 'Orange Hall in the Wood'. The Prince occupied himself actively with the project, even poring over the plans in his army camp. It was to be a homely place, the only concession to grandeur being a hall with an elevation of two storeys, which was intended for the picture collection of the Princess. The great octagonal hall that materialized was truly splendid with its arched roof and glass cupola surmounted by a glittering gilt coronet. The exotic woods of the floor must have been worth a fortune. The villa was tranquil without being remote from The Hague and it had all the makings of a delightful retreat. As it happened, things turned out differently from what the Prince and Princess had hoped.

36. HUIS TEN BOSCH
THE ORANGE HALL

The House in the Wood was nearing its completion and a gifted artist had already painted the portrait of Princess Amalia on a medallion in the cupola when Prince Frederick Henry died.

The portrait was replaced by another showing the lively princess in widow's weeds. The octagonal hall is decorated with murals, painted in an allegorical and heroic style rarely seen in this country, expressing the posthumous homage of a devoted wife. With the death of her husband, the villa had lost much of its attraction for Princess Amalia and it seemed appropriate that it should become a memorial to him. The Flemish artist Jordaens was commissioned to paint the murals exalting the life and deeds of Prince Frederick Henry. The paintings have added to the significance of the 17th-century architectural gem.

At present Huis ten Bosch is chiefly used for holding court levees and receiving royal visitors. The State Apartments, which include delightful 18th-century Chinese and Japanese rooms and a charming all-white stuccoed dining-room, are open to the public when the Royal family are not in residence. The House was a favourite retreat of several queens of Holland. Queen Wilhelmina liked to paint in the seclusion of the wisteria-covered loggia on the rare occasions she could escape from her official duties. The beautiful garden was the silver wedding-gift of the nation to Queen Juliana and Prince Bernhard. The Hague's reputation as an international centre for peace and negotiation was established when Queen Wilhelmina made Huis ten Bosch available for the first Peace Conference that was called in 1899.

37. HUIS TEN BOSCH
THE GARDEN FRONT

Well-heeled Dutchmen found a new territory to erect their palatial dwellings when a large part of the palace gardens was made available for residential development in the middle of the previous century. The king himself took an active interest in the planning of the new Willemspark area that was named in his honour.

The spacious houses stood in their own grounds and were surrounded by formal gardens with characteristic white shingle paths. And if they were not particularly handsome, they certainly had dignity and style. The large, rambling houses are practically uninhabitable today. Most of them are no longer private residences and are presently occupied by embassies, banks, and other institutions who keep up the style of the once exclusive residential district.

The monument on the oval which is the centre of the Willemspark area commemorates the restoration of independence, in 1813, at the end of the Napoleonic era. It is a typical example of the sculptured groups of allegorical and historical figures in dramatic attitudes which were much admired in the 19th century. The figures are actually not that old. The originals were made, in 1860, by a new process in which they were modelled in zinc on an iron framework and galvanized. But the thin copper coating and the zinc layer have worn away in the course of the century. The figures have therefore been cast anew in durable bronze.

38. ALEXANDER STREET
with the National Monument
on 'Plein 1813'

In the early years of this century The Hague developed at a phenomenal rate. Between the town proper and Scheveningen on the coast new districts sprang up overnight in an extravagantly decorated style of wide currency at the turn of the century. Mansard roofs, cupolas, pinnacles, wind-vanes, rose windows, balconies, loggias — the whole gamut of architectural fancy was represented.

Large houses were constructed in a combination of brick and sandstone, with arched roofs and a great deal of ornamental fretwork in wood and stone emphasizing the affluence of owners. The windows were tall and large in the 17th-century tradition that prevailed in this country, but the architectural style continued from the romantic manner, incorporating oriental and classical elements, to the no less romantic Art Nouveau which employed plant forms, animal and human figures, in an exotic linear style.

The large-scale development of the period was doubtless responsible for the manifold manifestations of Art Nouveau at The Hague. Apart from the luxury districts, the style also made its appearance in the intimate little shopping streets in the town centre. Trade was favourably influenced by the general prosperity and this was reflected in large show-windows and entire shop-fronts in fantastic constructions of steel and glass.

39. 'JUGENDSTIL'
(ART NOUVEAU) —
a pre-eminently Hague style

When The Hague reached the peak of its popularity as a shopping centre, the three-armed shopping arcade known as the Passage was constructed by a Belgian firm in the heart of the town.

A covered promenade is a boon in bad weather but more important even is the intimacy that makes shopping such fun. And since shoppers are practically inside already, they have less inhibitions about stepping into the stores. The absence of vehicles of any kind adds to the attraction. Shoppers stroll about and window-gaze at leisure. Town-planners have cottoned on to this again quite recently. The arcade at The Hague is now surrounded by shopping precincts where pedestrians can move about freely from store to store and from one promenade to another unhampered by traffic.

The Hague has a reputation of long standing for the profusion of beautiful and sophisticated objects on display in its stores. Display in every sense is the key-word. The nobles who assisted at the pageants of court and state in days gone by were discriminating patrons. They were only satisfied with the best that money could buy and their demands inevitably influenced the quality and range of merchandise in the Hague stores which attracted luxury lovers from all over the country. At present The Hague is practically a by-word in the fashionable world of Holland.

40. DE PASSAGE
The Shopping Arcade

The Hague is pervaded by the atmosphere of the sea, which is just beyond the horizon. Fascinated by an atmosphere and a horizon strange to the alps, a Swiss photographer once spent a solid fortnight shooting photos on the coast.

This may be a rather extreme example. But even less sensitive souls are subconsciously influenced by atmosphere and surroundings. A seaside holiday has a wonderfully bracing effect on inland dwellers, who may not be able to suppress a slight envy of Hague flat-dwellers with their magnificent views from top-storey flats of the sea beyond the dunes. — As a result of extensive developments during the past twenty-five years, The Hague's town-plan shows a large rectangle with one of the long sides running parallel to the coast. The most coveted residential estates are situated in this area.

The blocks of flats shown in the illustration are situated in the extreme south-west of The Hague. The rather isolated suburban villas surrounded by sandy wastes of pre-war days are now incorporated in the town. Developments are in hand to create resort amenities such as a promenade and extensive parking facilities to enhance the attraction of the wide sandy beaches.

41. New Urban Development in the Dunes

In the minds of many people Holland conjures up visions of wind-mills with turning sails, which drain the waterlogged land. In actual fact, most of the windmills in town and countryside are fondly cherished delightful anachronisms.

You are bound to run into one or two windmills amid The Hague's tall apartment houses. Standing by the waterside, with tarred wood and thatch spick and span, they are really no more than souvenirs. But they are kept in perfect working order even though it is more than likely that the surrounding buildings will take the wind out of their sails. In fact the municipality have one of their windmills working a statutory number of hours a year so as not to forfeit their milling rights.

Like so many other towns in Holland, The Hague is partly situated on polderland. Pumping-stations at strategic points automatically regulate the waterlevel in these low-lying areas to prevent flooding. In several instances these stations have been discreetly installed in old windmills. Real windmill fans — and there are many of them in the country — do not approve of this. They would rather preserve the windmills intact as a stand-by in case of failure of the powerful diesel-electric pumping-engines now in general use. In such a contingency, though, the windmills encapsulated in the residential areas which have usurped their native polders will hardly be able to play a role of any significance. They are preserved nevertheless because they are such a re-assuringly familiar, integral part of the Dutch land- and townscape.

42. A WINDMILL
caught up in the town

The First Peace Conference, called at The Hague in 1899, proposed the establishment of a Peace Palace in the town that had served the cause of peace by creating a favourable climate for the pacific settlement of international disputes.

The First Hague Conference, convened by Tsar Nicholas II of Russia, was held at Huis ten Bosch Palace which was placed at the disposal of the attending nations by Queen Wilhelmina. Peace by negotiation was their aim. A Permanent Court of International Justice was established, which now operates as the International Court of Justice under the Charter of the United Nations.

The idea of the Peace Palace fired the imagination of the American steel magnate Andrew Carnegie who donated a sum of one and a half million dollars towards its realization. The Dutch government provided a suitable site and announced a competition for a design. Forty-six nations contributed materials and decorations which were typical for their countries; Germany the ornamental railings, Norway and Sweden the granite of the balconies, Belgium the bronze doors, Italy the marble in the hall, England magnificent stained-glass windows, Denmark a porcelain fountain, Switzerland the tower-clock, Japan embroidered wall-hangings, and the Tsar a jasper vase weighing three tons. The result was the most lavishly decorated edifice in all Holland.

All the symbolism and sympathy could unfortunately not prevent the outbreak of the First World War only a year after the completion of the sumptuous palace dedicated to peace, nor avert the Second two decades later. Though World Peace, the avowed aim of the Founders, is presently greeted with scepticism in many circles, the Hague Peace Palace is more than a vain gesture. It is the seat of a body committed to the advancement of international justice and it is a tangible expression of the desire for peace that lives in all nations.

43. HET VREDESPALEIS
THE PEACE PALACE

One of the major attractions of The Hague is the model town of Madurodam which has acquired quite an international reputation. Its name rings a bell with many people who know little or nothing of The Hague or even of Holland.

See Madurodam and do Holland in an hour! There may be just a grain of truth in this remark ascribed to an American visitor-in-a-hurry. For Madurodam is a true-to-life miniature Dutch town with canals and bridges, houses, factories and industrial estates, surrounded by polders. The houses are scale replicas (1/25) of historical landmarks and other important buildings, ancient and modern, from all parts of the country. There are bulbfields on the outskirts, also to scale, and real trees carefully kept down in size. Harbours, airport, motor roads, rail- and tramways running to schedule, a street fair — it's all there. Organ music issues from a church and the barrel-organ produces an authentic sound. — Madurodam certainly rates a visit, witness the thousands of delighted visitors who flock there every season. But it's a mistake to think that a model town can ever be a substitute for the real thing. Its streets may be full of miniature people but when all's said and done, it's meeting real people that helps us understand what makes any place tick.

44. MADURODAM
THE MODEL TOWN

One of the largest buildings erected in this country in recent years, the Netherlands Congress Centre, is a complex of conference rooms catering for 9,000 people. The Hague is justly proud of the magnificent centre of cultural activities.

In the last few decades conferences have become an accepted medium of international communication and it is a matter of sound common-sense to provide the necessary facilities. Well-equipped congress centres have in fact been built in most towns of any importance in recent years. The size of the Hague Centre is a measure of the international function it is expected to fulfil and of its importance as a civic centre. With the anticipated increase in leisure time, larger groups of the population will be participating in cultural events in the future.

The large foyer and roomy corridors with various shops and stands form a network of lanes between the assembly rooms, and in reception rooms on all floors people have ample opportunity for meeting. These built-in amenities are essential elements of modern congress centres, for personal contact between delegates is no less important than the scholarly address one has come to hear.

On the other hand, one does wonder whether the enormous sums invested in these centres are justified, whether this passion for conventions is not just a passing fad. The following statement by a distinguished academic allays our doubts on this score: "If I were to rely on my own resources to keep up with international developments in my particular subject, I would be spending all my time in travel and study. Now I attend one or two conferences a year, in a fortnight's time I have the opportunity of talking to everybody who's anybody in my field, and we are informed about recent advances in papers read by our leading men. In the Middle Ages correspondence with distant colleagues was indispensable to scholars; now this applies to conferences."

45. HET CONGRESGEBOUW
THE NETHERLANDS
CONGRESS CENTRE

The large foyer of the Congress Centre is a contemporary version of the marketplace. With all meeting-rooms opening onto it at several levels, it is the focal point of the activities. The information desk controls the traffic, directing the stream of visitors to their destinations.

The Centre was built to the design of the architect J. J. P. Oud. The structural problems posed by the vast span of the foyer, which is unsupported by piers, were solved by adopting engineering techniques only employed previously in damming the estuaries of the large rivers in the Delta project. The Congress Centre is the largest of its kind in Western Europe. It has a volume of 290,000 cubic metres, which is eight times as large as its by no means undersized neighbour, the Municipal Museum. Also for the record: five million bricks were required for the building; the wiring laid end to end would stretch from The Hague to Marseilles; 4,000 square metres of glass keep window-cleaners busy. The great hall (which seats 2,000) serves as the permanent concert hall of The Hague's civic orchestra, the Residentie Orkest, which is one of the leading orchestras of the country.

The Centre's amenities include a large restaurant, several bars, and hotel accomodation for congress organizers who need to spend some time here in advance. These suites are situated in the tall triangular tower which is a handy beacon for delegates who go roaming in town. A hotel has been built in the grounds of the Congress Centre.

46. CONGRESS CENTRE
THE FOYER

Once a year, on the third Tuesday in September, the Gold Coach winds its way through the streets of The Hague, bearing the Queen in state from the Palace on Lange Voorhout to the Binnenhof.

The Royal family shun the undue display of pomp and ceremony which creates a distance between sovereign and subjects. But the royal procession, in which the Gold Coach figures prominently, on the occasion of the annual opening of the States General by the Queen is a time-honoured tradition.

The gilded and painted coach, embellished with allegorical figures and scenes, was presented to Queen Juliana's mother Queen Wilhelmina on her accession to the throne, in 1898, by the citizens of Amsterdam. The coach was specially constructed to negotiate narrow archways and streets, for it was the young Queen's wish that she should not be debarred from driving in any part of the town.

In a sense the ornate seventy-year-old vehicle is an antiquated phenomenon but it exercises a powerful attraction for all that. There are always thousands of people watching the brilliant annual spectacle: the Queen and Prince Consort in the Gold Coach with its team of eight and gaily liveried coachman, grooms and footmen, the princesses in open calashes, the military escorts and bands in full-dress uniform. The full pageantry of state adds a touch of poetry to the cool neutrality of modern democracy.

47. ROYAL PROCESSION
with the Gold Coach